To Patricia Hoov

As a kindergarten teacher,
you noticed something in me when I was very young.
All my life, you encouraged and nurtured me
in your own very wise and tender way.
I am deeply grateful!

(Had I thought of it in time,
someone in this book would be reading a cereal box!)

All my love,

Robbie

To Lydia ~
Enjoy the journey
the Lord is
unfolding for you!
RJGuy

Illustrations by yami-digital

Cover design by John Weisman

First Printing, 2020
Printed in the United States of America

In our house I'm right at home!

So as my legs begin to roam

each day is like another quest

exploring the places I know best!

Around our house you carry me

from room to room so I can see

the places where we live each day,

and where we eat and sleep and play!

When you lift me way up high

different places catch my eye,

and when you set me on the floor

I discover even more!

In our living room we do

so many things the whole day through!

We talk and dance, play hide and seek

and laugh when one of us sneaks a peek!

There's the couch where we watch TV,

and the chair where you often read to me!

And hanging there up on the wall

are lots of pictures of us all!

I crawl through the kitchen door

to look and touch and to explore

the drawers and shelves and storage spaces,

where all our dishes have their places!

There's the fridge where we keep my drink,

and your hiding place above the sink,

the table where we always eat,

and where I sit in my special seat!

The rooms upstairs are where we sleep,

and there's the closet where I keep

my shirts and pants, and where my shoes

are all lined up in pairs of twos!

My books are stacked upon the shelf

beside my bed, where by myself

I sometimes nap and sometimes play

or sleep until it's another day!

Then I awake and we start again—

all these adventures have no end!

Living together with your familiar faces

makes our house one of my favorite places!